THE BEST CHRISTMAS SUPER JUMBO COLORING BOOK

CREATIVE CHILD PRESS is a trademark of Playmore Inc., Publishers and Waldman Publishing Corp., New York, New York

Playmore, Inc. Publishers
Under arrangement with Waldman Publishing Corp.
New York, New York

The Best Snowman

SNOWMAN CONTEST COME ONE COME ALL!

"I'm going to make a snowman for the Snowman Contest," says little Christmas Bear.

"We are, too," says Bear's friends.
"Let's go. We don't want to be late," they say.

Everyone arrives just in time . . .

. . . to hear that the best snowman will win a prize.

With three round buttons, this snowman is dressed with great care by the animal in the plaid cap—Bertie Bear.

Which one will win? Will it be tall or short?
Will it be fat or thin?

And all of a sudden, what should appear, but a
tumbling ball of snow out of thin air . . .

"Oh, can I help?" asked Christmas Bear.

"We're almost done," said Mother.
"But you can have the broken pieces."

The next morning, Christmas Bear found popcorn on the
floor. He scooped it up and put it in his special bag.

In the afternoon, everyone went out to gather
pine branches . . .

Christmas Bear took all the holly and pine that was
not used and ran outside with his special bag.

"What has Christmas Bear made?"
the Bear family wondered.

"Why, it's wonderful—a Christmas tree for the birds."
You have the best Christmas spirit of all, Christmas bear!

Santa Claus gets lots of mail at the North Pole.

Santa's elves help sort the letters.

Santa Claus reads every single letter.

Mrs. Claus helps Santa hang mistletoe
above the doorway.

It's time to decorate the Christmas tree.

Draw a line connecting each pair of objects that go together.

Santa checks the path he will take
on a giant map.

"HO! HO! HO! It's time for my midnight ride!"
Santa says.

S.Claus

Up, up, up they go!

Santa Claus is coming to town.

"This house is my first stop!"

With the help of two tiny elves,
Santa's sleigh lands on the rooftop.

Down the chimney Santa goes.

He lands at the bottom with a big "thump"!

First, Santa fills up all the stockings.

Then he takes time out for a snack.

"Everybody here has been good so I'll leave
lots of toys," Santa says . . .

drawing lesson

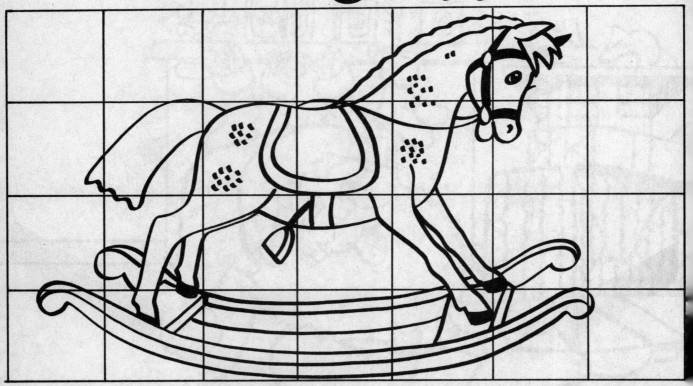

Draw the rocking horse in the squares below.

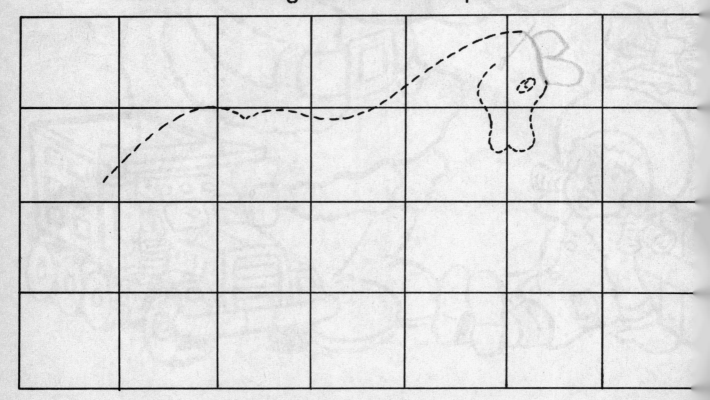

LOOK-ALIKES

Find the matching pair of soldiers.

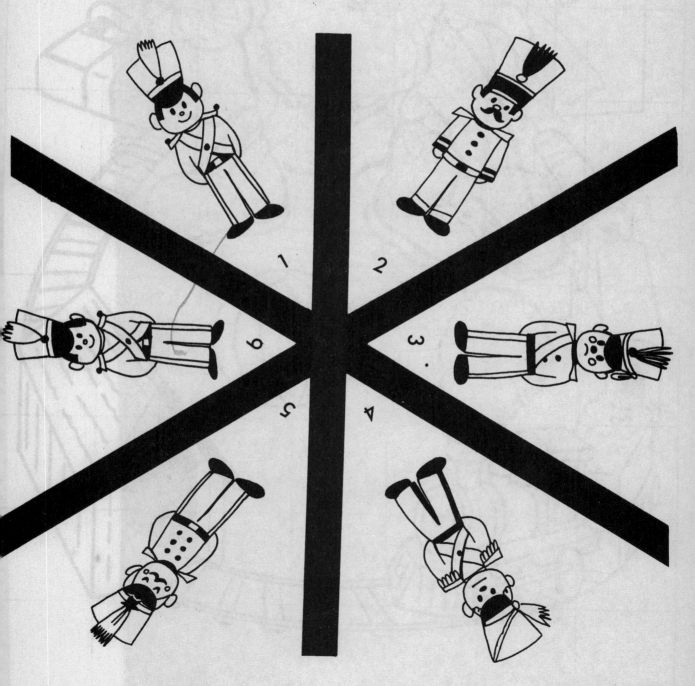

Next, Santa sets up a shiny new train se

Santa hides behind a chair.

"Oh, boy! Santa's been here!"

"Now it's time for me to leave."

Up on the rooftop the elves are waiting.

Santa pops out of the chimney.

Off they go to deliver toys to good
little girls and boys.

Santa stops at house after house,
and soon his work is done.

"Merry Christmas to all and to all
a good night!"

Scrambled Pictures

How many puppies can you find?

Santa's Letters

"Hi, Christmas Bear. Since you know Santa Claus,
would you take my letter to him?"

"That's a great idea. We'll give you
our letters, too."

Everyone in town hears that Christmas Bear
is going to the North Pole . . .

. . . and they all line up with letters for Santa.

CAN YOU GET THROUGH THIS FUNNY HAND-PUPPET MAZE?

LOOK-ALIKES

Find the matching pair of baby dolls.

Oh, boy. Christmas Bear has tons of mail for Santa.

. . . and off he goes.

Christmas Bear is getting so tired . . .

. . . he simply can't take another step with all
the letters and the big jar of honey.

LOOK AND TELL

Name and circle the things which are sweet.

Name and circle the things that move on wheels.

LOOK-ALIKES

Find the matching pair of snowmen.

"Well, this is no problem at all," Christmas Bear says.
"I'll just eat all the honey . . .

... and put the letters in the empty honey jar."

In no time at all . . .

"These are the sweetest letters I've ever read."

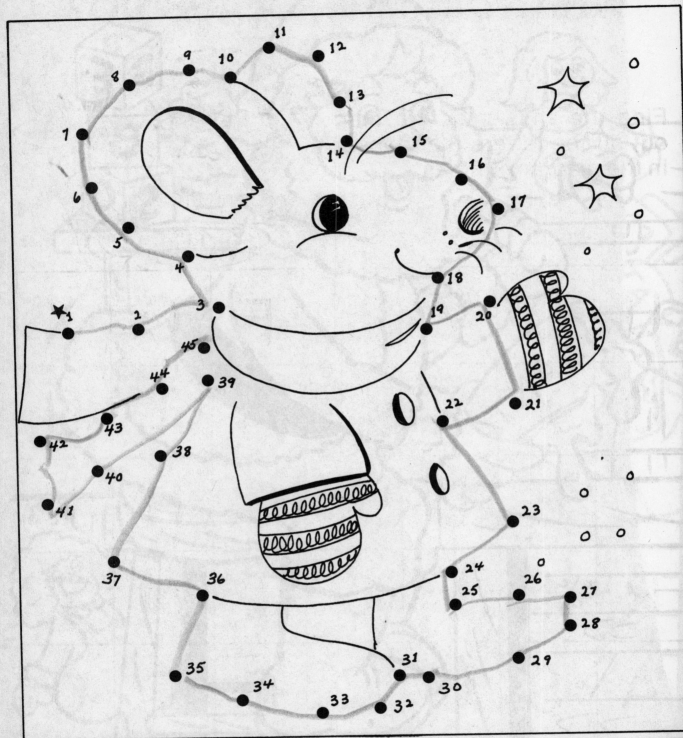

FOLLOW THE DOTS

Morris Mouse's Mother Made him some Matching Mittens!

WHAT DID MRS. CLAUS DO?

Find the answer by crossing out all the letters that appear in the diagram 4 times.

U	D	Z	E	F	C	X
O	X	R		A	T	U
Z	E	D	X	C	H	X
R	I	F	S	T	M	Z
A	S	U	C	O	F	O
F	U	K	Z	I	E	S

Melanie and Matthew are the luckiest
kids in the world.

They've been invited to the North Pole to spend an old-fashioned Christmas with Santa Claus!

The ride in Santa's sleigh is very exciting.

Melanie makes a wish upon a star and Matthew looks
down at their pretty little town.

At long last the sleigh lands
at the North Pole.

"HO! HO! HO! Welcome! Welcome!" Santa
laughs with glee.

"It's really Santa Claus!" Matthew
can hardly believe it.

Inside the house Mrs. Claus is
busy baking cookies.

The children have a delicious snack before
visiting Santa's workshop.

"These gingerbread men are delicious, Mrs. Claus,"
Melanie says.

Christmas Cookies

How many of Mrs. Claus' hidden baking ingredients can you find?

EGGS MILK FLOUR BUTTER SUGAR SALT VANILLA

COLOR BY NUMBER

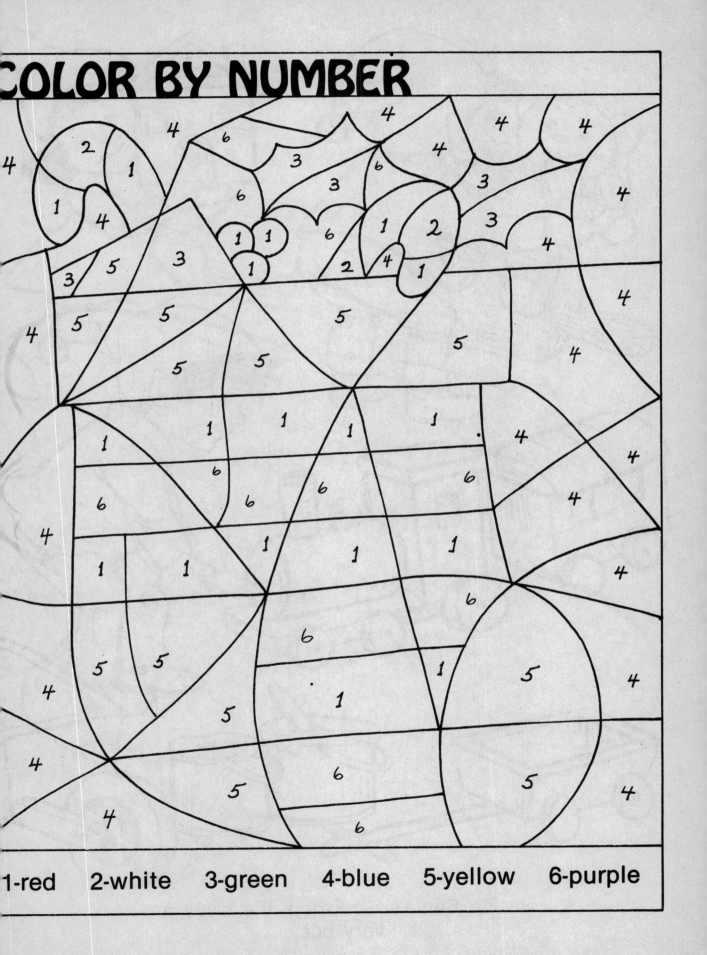

1-red   2-white   3-green   4-blue   5-yellow   6-purple

Inside Santa's workshop, the elves are
very busy.

"And now it's time to find a big, beautiful
Christmas tree," Santa says . . .

. . . as Mrs. Claus helps the children get dressed
to go outside.

Santa drives his sleigh deep into the woods.

"There's a perfect Christmas tree, Santa!"
Melanie says.

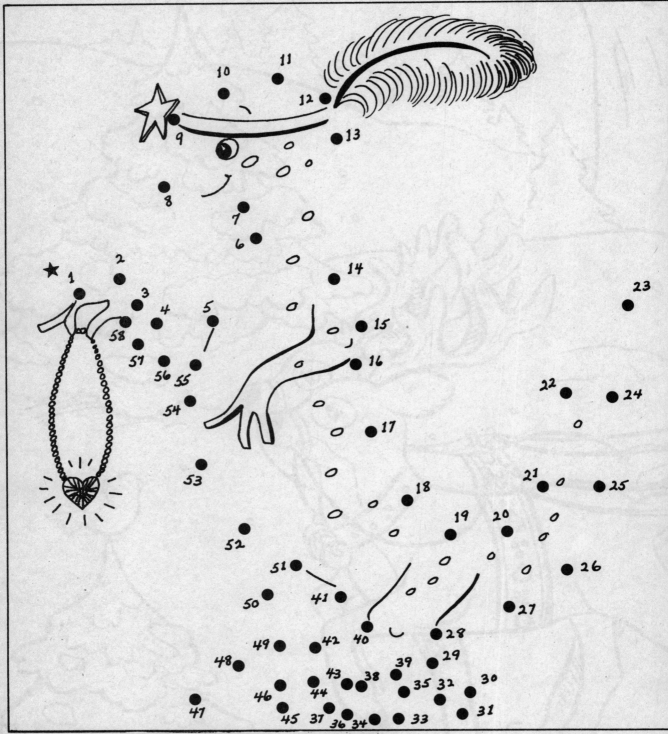

FOLLOW THE DOTS

**Nellie Newt got what she wanted for Christmas —
a Nice New Necklace!**

find the 6 differences

These pictures look alike, but look again. Can you find 6 places where they are different?

Melanie and Matthew build a jolly snowman while Santa's elf puts the Christmas tree in the sleigh.

"It's time to leave," says Santa.

"Ho! Ho! Ho! We're back, Mrs. Claus.
Do you like the tree we found?"

"It's beautiful, and we'll have such
fun decorating it!"

Inside the house Melanie helps string
some popcorn . . .

. . . while Matthew and Mrs. Claus tie bright red ribbons on gingerbread ornaments.

Everyone helps decorate the tree.

"I think it's the nicest Christmas tree
we've ever had," Santa says.

COLD THINGS

How many cold things can you find?

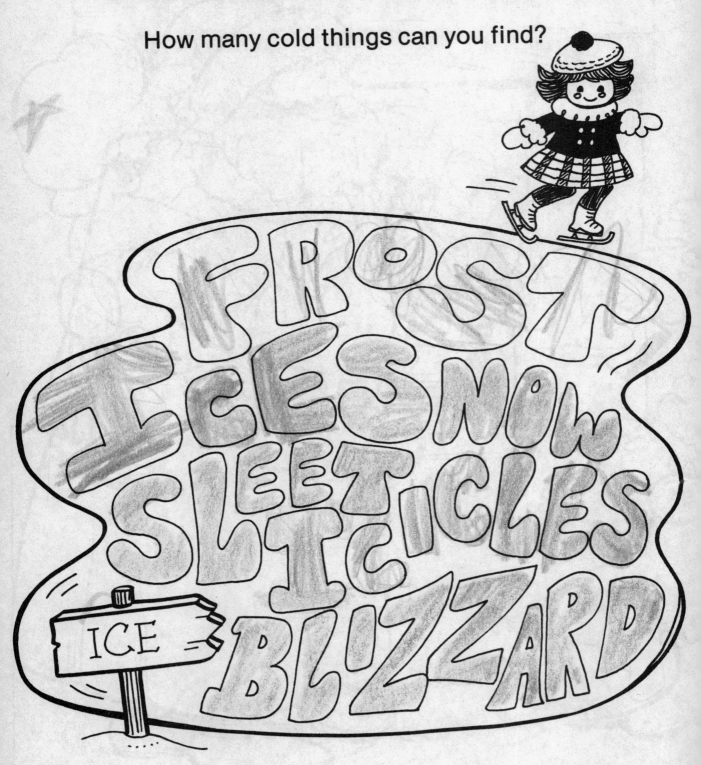

FROST ICE SNOW SLEET ICICLES BLIZZARD

ICE

WARM THINGS

How many nice warm things can you find?

"It's time for good boys and girls
to go to sleep!"

Santa places gifts under the tree.

"Hooray! It's Christmas Day!"

"Which present should we open first?"
Matthew wonders.

Santa and Mrs. Claus watch the children
open their gifts.

"Isn't Christmas the very best time of the year?" says Mrs. Claus.

"This is just what I wanted!" Matthew says.

Melanie loves her new dollhouse.

Matthew has a present for Santa—
it's a brand-new hat . . .

. . . and Melanie gives Mrs. Claus a
beautiful apron.

Everyone has fun . . .

. . . playing with the Christmas toys!

"It's time for Christmas dinner," says Santa
as he rings the dinner bell.

Mrs. Claus takes the Christmas turkey out
of the oven.

The table is piled high with lots
of Christmas goodies . . .

. . . and everything smells simply delicious.

Matthew and Melanie each eat a
Christmas turkey drumstick.